DRESSING UP!

DRESSING UP!

50 Step-by-Step Amazing Outfits to Make and Faces to Paint

Petra Boase, with face painting by Bettina Graham
Photographs by John Freeman

ARMADILLO

This edition is published by Armadillo, an imprint of
Anness Publishing Ltd, Blaby Road, Wigston,
Leicestershire LE18 4SE; info@anness.com

www.annesspublishing.com

If you like the images in this book and would like to investigate
using them for publishing, promotions or advertising, please visit
our website www.practicalpictures.com for more information.

© Anness Publishing Ltd 2013

Publisher: Joanna Lorenz
Series Editor: Lindsay Porter
Designers: Peter Laws and Lucy Doncaster
Photographer: John Freeman
Production Controller: Mai-Ling Collyer

PUBLISHER'S NOTE
Although the advice and information in this book are believed
to be accurate and true at the time of going to press, neither
the authors nor the publisher can accept any legal responsibility
or liability for any errors or omissions that may have been made
nor for any inaccuracies nor for any loss, harm or injury that
comes about from following instructions or advice in this book.

Manufacturer: Anness Publishing Ltd, Blaby Road, Wigston,
Leicestershire LE18 4SE, England
For Product Tracking go to: www.annesspublishing.com/tracking
Batch: 6904-22668-1127

CONTENTS

Introduction 6
Materials and Equipment 8
Face Painting Materials 10

Techniques 12
Making a Waistband 12
Covering a Button 12
Decorative Stitches 13
Making Your Own Pantaloons 13
Papier-mâché 14
Tracing a Template 14
Applying Eye Make-up and
Handling the Brush 15
Applying a Base 16
Shading 16
Lips 17
Ageing the Face 17
Removing Make-up 17

Animals 18
Making a Tail 18
Making Ears 19
Cat 20
Animal Collar 22

Animal Accessories 23
Tiger 24
Lion 26
Spotted Dog 28
Rabbit 29
Bumble Bee 30
Butterfly 32
Mouse 33
Owl 34
Monkey 36
Panda 37

Ghouls, Ghosts and Monsters 38
Witch 38
Ghost 40
Egyptian Mummy 41
Vampire 42
Martian 44
Frankenstein's Monster 46
Purple Monster 47
Skeleton 48
Zombie 50
Gremlin 51
Dinosaur 52

Fun and Fantasy Figures 54
Clown 54
Ballerina 56

Fairy 57
Scarecrow 58
Angel 60
Devil 61
Robot 62
Astronaut 64
Sunflower 66
Pumpkin 68
Carrot 70
Genie 72
Dragon 74

Pirates, Princes and Other People 76
Gypsy 76
Cowboy 78
Native American 79
Pirate 80
Prince 82
Princess 83
Hippy 84
Knight 86
Wizard 87
Super Hero 88
Super Heroine 89

Templates 90

Index 96

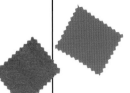

INTRODUCTION

Whether you are having a party, putting on a play or just having fun at home, dressing up and face painting provide great excitement and lots of laughs.

There are all sorts of different costume and face painting ideas for you to choose from in the book, but remember to read the instructions first and allow yourself enough time to make the costume. You don't want to be turning up to a party or performing in a play wearing a costume that is only half made!

In order to keep the costumes as inexpensive as possible, spend time looking in second-hand stores and flea markets for old clothes and fabric. These can then be cut up or altered according to the costume. Fabric paints are very useful if you wish to design your own patterns and motifs, but remember to read the instructions properly before using them.

Before you start the face painting, make sure that your model is sitting comfortably and has a towel wrapped around his or her shoulders to protect his or her clothes. Keep any loose hair off the face with a headband or a few hair clips. It is also a good idea to lay out all your paints and equipment on a table that is close by and have a mirror at hand so that your model can see how the design is evolving.

When you have finished making a costume or face painting, remember to clean up all your equipment and tidy it away neatly.

Materials and Equipment

*These are a selection of the materials used in this book.
If you can't find exactly the same materials, see if there
is anything else you could substitute.*

Adhesive tape
This strong tape can be used for fastening heavy materials. It also can be used for decoration.

Baubles
These can be used to decorate headdresses and other accessories. Only use baubles made from plastic or paper.

Braid
This comes in a range of styles and widths and can be used to decorate clothes and accessories.

Buttons
Interesting buttons can be used as decoration.

Covered elastic cord
This can be purchased from department stores and comes in different shades and strengths. It can be attached to hats to make them easier to wear.

Crêpe and tissue paper sheets
These can be used for decoration. They are quite fragile and are best suited to costumes that will only need to be worn once or twice.

Feathers
These can be bought from sewing stores and can be used to decorate hats and accessories.

Felt
This comes in a range of shades. It is easy to cut and won't fray.

Foil
This can be cut up or crumpled to create different decorative effects.

Garden canes
Paint and decorate one and turn it into a fairy's wand, or use several ones painted green as the stems on a bunch of paper flowers.

Glitter
This can be glued on as decoration. If there is any left be sure to pour it back into the tube to use again.

Headbands
These can be decorated to make a headdress or covered in fur to make a pair of ears.

Hessian (burlap)
This heavy cloth is perfect for costumes. When cut, the cloth may be frayed to make a fringe.

Metal kitchen scourers
These are made of soft metal and are used in the kitchen but they also make fun decorations.

Milliner's wire
This is covered with thread and is safer to use than ordinary wire. You should still take care with the sharp ends, and cover them with tape.

Netting
This fabric is perfect for making light, airy skirts and wings. It is available in a wide range of shades from fabric stores.

Newspaper
Save old newspaper and use to protect surfaces when you are working or to make pâpier-maché.

Paintbrushes
Use a range of different sizes to apply paint and glue.

Paints
Use non-toxic paints to add details.

Paper in various shades
Heavy paper can be used for making hats and headdresses.

Press studs (snap fasteners)
These are quick to add to a costume.

Ribbons
These come in a wide range and can be used for making bows.

Safety pins
These can be taped on to the back of badges or used to help thread elastic through a waistband.

Sewing thread
It is a good idea to match your sewing thread to your main material.

String
String can be used as a fastener on an outfit, or used for hanging pendants.

Supermarket packaging
Boxes, egg cartons, and plastic and foil containers can all be used to make and decorate costumes.

Tinsel
Save spare tinsel and use it to create sparkly accessories and details.

Wool (yarn)
This can be used for making wigs and braids.

feathers

egg carton

Christmas bauble

metal kitchen scourer

netting

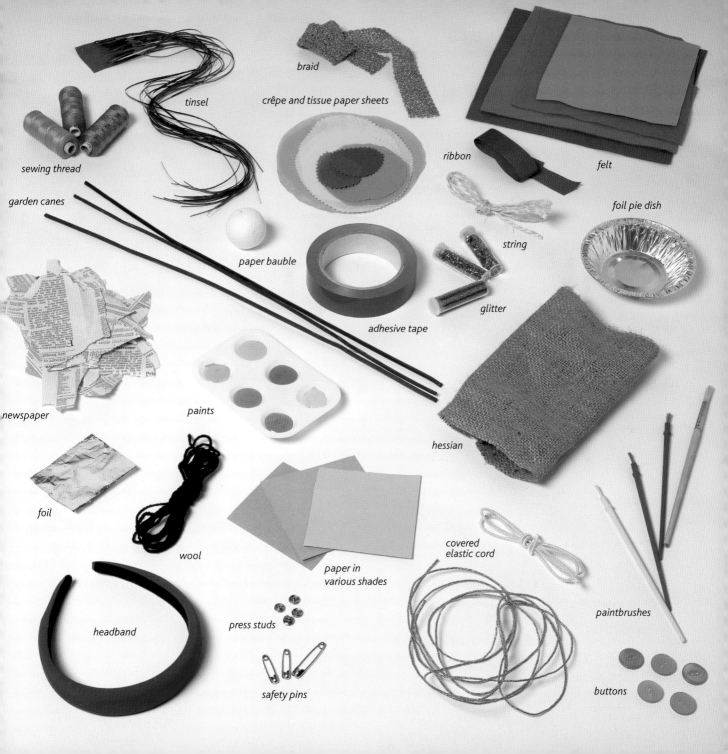

braid

crêpe and tissue paper sheets

tinsel

ribbon

felt

sewing thread

garden canes

string

foil pie dish

paper bauble

adhesive tape

glitter

newspaper

paints

hessian

foil

wool

paper in various shades

covered elastic cord

paintbrushes

headband

press studs

safety pins

buttons

Face Painting Materials

There is a huge selection of face-painting materials available at a range of different prices. Toy and novelty stores often stock face paints, as well as theatrical suppliers.

Child's make-up kit
This is a good starter set. It usually includes a bright range of face paints, sponges, brushes, and a well for water. It is available from most toy stores.

Cleansing towels
These are ideal for removing the last traces of face paint.

Cold cream cleanser
Even though most water-based face paints come off with soap and water, you can also use a cream cleanser with soft tissues or cotton wool balls.

Cotton swabs
These are used to apply and remove make-up around the eye.

Eyebrow brush
This is used for combing eyebrows and eyelashes.

Fake blood
This is great for special effects and can be purchased from theatrical and novelty stores.

Glitter gel
This comes in a range of shades and gives a sparkly finish. It can be purchased from costume stores.

Make-up brushes
These come in a range of sizes and shapes. It is a good idea to have different types to use for different effects. Wide brushes either have a flat or rounded edge and are used for large areas of decorating or for applying blusher, highlights or all-over powder. Medium brushes with a rounded edge are useful for shaping shaded areas, while narrow brushes, either flat or pointed, are used for outlining and painting fine details and lips.

Make-up fixative
This is available from professional theatrical stores. It fixes the make up, therefore making it last longer. Make sure the model's eyes are closed when spraying it.

Make-up palette
This provides a range of solid, vibrant shades that give very good effects. You can mix tones together if the set you have doesn't provide the range of shades you require.

Make-up pencils
These are used for drawing fine details on the face. They can also be used for outlining your basic design, if necessary.

Make-up pots
These are purchased from specialist theatrical stores. They are more expensive but are excellent quality and come in a wonderful range of shades.

Plastic palette
Use as a surface for mixing face paints together to achieve more subtle tones.

Soft tissue
Use with a dab of cold cream cleanser to remove make-up, or for wiping off any excess make-up from your brush.

Sponges
Covered sponges such as powder puffs are used for applying dry powders. Cellulose or latex sponges can be used slightly damp to give an even shade. Stipple sponges are made from soft plastic and are used for creating textured effects such as beard growth, animal skins and other effects.

Temple white
This is available from theatrical stores and is applied to the hair to give an aged effect.

Wax make-up crayons
If you do not mind a less professional finish, these are a good, inexpensive option. They give a less solid tone and the result is less long-lasting but they are often formulated for young children to use themselves.

fine make-up brushes

medium make-up brushes

make-up p•

eyebrow brush•

make-up fixative

cleansing towels

child's make-up kit

cold cream cleanser

fake blood

make-up palette

make-up pots

temple white

cotton swabs

plastic palette

sponges

soft tissue

wax make-up crayons

glitter gel

wide make-up brushes

TECHNIQUES

Making a Waistband

Elasticated waistbands make all costumes easy to put on and take off.

YOU WILL NEED
sewing needle and thread or
   sewing machine
safety pin
elastic

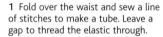

1 Fold over the waist and sew a line of stitches to make a tube. Leave a gap to thread the elastic through.

2 Attach a safety pin to the end of the elastic and thread it through the tube until it comes out the other end.

3 Pull the two ends of elastic to gather the waist to the right size and tie a knot. Sew up the opening in the tube.

Covering a Button

By covering buttons you can choose your own fabric to match the outfit. The clown costume includes lots of buttons.

YOU WILL NEED
fabric
scissors
self-cover button
sewing needle and thread

1 Cut out a circle of fabric twice as wide as the button. Sew a line of running stitches around the the edge of circle.

2 Open the button and place the front on the circle of fabric. Pull the threads to gather them up around the button.

3 Place the back on the button.

Decorative Stitches

These stitches can add a finishing touch to an outfit, whether adding bright details in thread, or sewing on fabric shapes.

YOU WILL NEED
sewing needle and thread

1 Running stitch is useful for sewing on patches and other shapes. You can make the stitches as long or as short as you like.

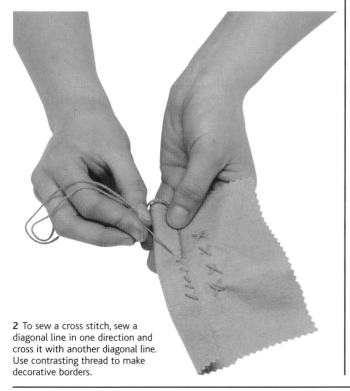

2 To sew a cross stitch, sew a diagonal line in one direction and cross it with another diagonal line. Use contrasting thread to make decorative borders.

Making Your Own Pantaloons

Decorate the pantaloons according to the character required. These basic pantaloons can be used for the pirate and genie costumes.

YOU WILL NEED
2m/2yds fabric
pattern, enlarged from the
    template section
scissors
sewing needle and thread
    or sewing machine
safety pin
elastic

1 Fold the fabric in half, with the right sides facing, and place the pattern on the fold of the fabric. Cut out two identical pieces. Keep each piece of the pantaloon folded in half with the right sides facing and sew along the inside leg with a 5mm/¼in seam allowance.

2 Turn one leg piece right side out and place it inside the other leg, matching up the raw edges. Stitch the two pieces together. Turn the legs right side out. Fold over the waist of the pantaloons and sew a double line of stitching to make a tube for the elastic to go through. Leave a gap to thread the elastic through. Do the same around the bottom of each pantaloon leg.

3 Attach the safety pin to one end of the elastic and tie a knot at the end. Thread the elastic through the tube. Do the same with each pantaloon leg. Sew up the gaps in the tubes.

Papier-mâché

*Pâpier-maché can be used for all kinds of things.
In this book it has been used to make adornments,
accessories and helmets.*

YOU WILL NEED
white glue
bowl
water
paintbrush
newspaper
cardboard cut in the shape you
    want to make, or a balloon
petroleum jelly (optional)

1 For the paste, pour some white
glue into a bowl and add water.
Mix the two together with a
paintbrush. The mixture should
not be too runny.

2 Tear up sheets of newspaper into
small pieces. Dip the pieces one at a
time into the glue and stick them on
to the cardboard shape.

3 Cover the cardboard shape with
about three layers of paper and
leave it to dry thoroughly. If you
are covering a balloon, apply water
or petroleum jelly to the surface
and then the layers of paper. This
will stop the shape sticking to the
balloon when you pop it.

Tracing a Template

*Some of the projects in this book use templates.
To transfer the template to a piece of cardboard
simply follow these instructions.*

YOU WILL NEED
tracing paper
soft pencil
cardboard or paper
scissors

1 Place a piece of tracing paper
over the template and draw around
the shape using a pencil. The outline
should be dark and heavy.

2 Take the tracing paper off the
template and turn it over. Rub over
the traced image with pencil on the
reverse side of the tracing paper.

3 Place the tracing paper on a piece
of cardboard or paper with the
rubbed pencil side facing down. Draw
over the lines to transfer the picture.

4 Carefully cut out the template,
and use as a pattern for costumes
or accessories.

Applying Eye Make-up and Handling the Brush

Successful face painting is all about being happy handling the brush. Practise brush strokes until you feel confident enough to attempt a complete design. If you are not satisfied with what you have done, simply remove the make-up with soap and water or a cream cleanser, and start again.

YOU WILL NEED
water-based face paints
fine make-up brush
tissue

1 Ask the model to close her eyes and paint a straight line across each eyelid. Ensure the brush is not too wet, and do not work too close to the eyelashes. If the make-up should get into the eyes, wash with warm water immediately. You may want to rest on the model to give you a steadier hand.

2 You can also support your hand on the model's cheek, resting on a piece of tissue to help you paint a smooth straight line. After some practice you will find out what is most comfortable for you.

3 When shading above the model's eye, the model should look down at the floor. You may need to wait a few minutes for the make-up to dry completely before moving on to the next stage.

4 When shading under the model's eye, support your hand on their cheek, resting on a piece of tissue. Ask the model to look up while you apply the make-up, and start at the inner corner of the eye.

5 Continue to the outer corner, making an even, sweeping motion beyond the outer corner of the eye. This will enhance the eyes, and give a dramatic finish.

Applying a Base

An evenly applied, well-shaded base is the foundation for successful face-painting effects. Experiment with different tones, blended directly on to the face, to change the model's appearance.

YOU WILL NEED
make-up sponge
water-based face paints

1 Using a damp sponge, begin to apply the base tone over the face. To avoid streaks or patchiness, make sure the sponge is not too wet.

2 Make sure the base tone is applied evenly over the face and fill in any patchy areas.

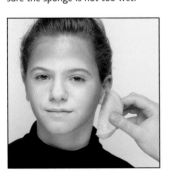

3 Using a contrasting shade, sponge around the edge of the face.

4 Blend the shades together for an even finish. Always make sure the base tones are dry before you start to decorate the face with other shades.

Shading

Shading can change the shape of your model's face dramatically.

YOU WILL NEED
powder face paints
soft make-up brush

1 When shading under the model's eyes, ask them to look up so that the area becomes smooth and easy to work on. This also stops the model from blinking as you work.

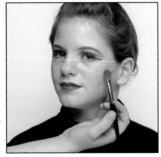

2 To exaggerate the shape of the model's face, shade each cheekbone with blusher or dark powder face paint.

3 To shade the whole face, use a large, soft brush.

Lips

YOU WILL NEED
fine lipstick brush
water-based face paints

1 Using a fine lipstick brush, paint the lips. Ask the model to close her mouth as this makes the muscles firmer and easier to outline. Ask the model to open her mouth to fill in the corners. You may need to wait a few seconds to allow the make-up to dry before going on to the next stage.

2 Rest your hand on the model's chin, on a piece of tissue or a powder puff. Paint an even outline around the lips. You may want to experiment with using a different shade for the outline, or extending the line beyond the natural curve of the model's mouth to create a different shape.

Ageing the Face

You can make even the young look very old with this technique.

YOU WILL NEED
water-based face paints
fine make-up brush
wide make-up brush

1 Ask the model to frown. This will show where lines will occur with age. Apply fine lines of make-up in these areas. Ask the model to smile, and apply a line starting at either side of the nose, down the fold of the cheek.

2 Ask your model to purse her lips, and apply fine lines around the mouth, within the natural folds.

3 Finish by giving a light dusting of a lighter base tone with a wide brush on the cheeks and temples.

Removing Make-up

Most face paints will come off with soap and water. If soap is too drying, or if some paint or make-up persists, you may want to remove make-up as follows.

YOU WILL NEED
cold cream cleanser
cotton wool ball or
   soft tissues

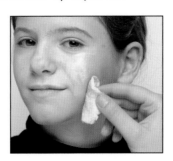

1 Pour the cream on to a damp cotton wool ball or tissue and gently rub the make-up off the face. Use a clean tissue or your fingers to apply more cold cream cleanser.

2 If liked, give a final cleanse with soap and water, and dry by patting the face with a soft towel.

ANIMALS

Making a Tail

This tail was made to go with the spotted dog outfit.
You can make a tail for a cat or tiger in the same way.

YOU WILL NEED
old pair of children's black tights
scissors
newspaper
elastic
sewing needle and thread
felt
fabric glue

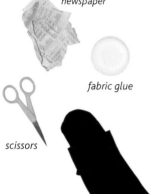

newspaper

fabric glue

scissors

tights

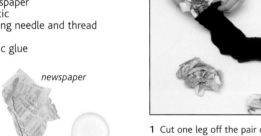

1 Cut one leg off the pair of tights. Scrunch up balls of newspaper and fill up the leg until it is quite firm.

2 Tie a knot at the end of the leg.

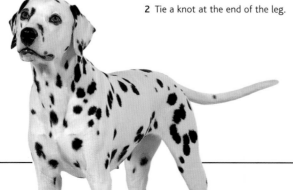

3 Measure your waist so you know how much elastic you need. Sew the elastic in a loop on to the knotted end of the tail.

4 This tail is for the spotted dog so it has been decorated with spots of felt glued on with fabric glue. You could always paint on a different design using fabric paints.

Making Ears

These ears add a cuddly touch to any of the animal outfits. You can adjust the size of the ears and choose material to suit the animal.

YOU WILL NEED
headband
tape measure
fake fur
scissors
sewing needle and thread
felt
fabric glue (optional)
template for ears
cardboard
pencil

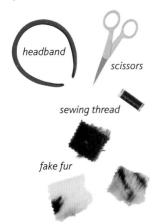

headband

scissors

sewing thread

fake fur

1 Measure the length of the headband with a tape measure. Cut out a piece of fur to fit, allowing an extra 2cm/1in at each end for folding over. Sew the fur on to the headband as shown.

2 Cut out a piece of felt to fit the inside of the headband and sew or glue it on. Trace the template on to a piece of cardboard.

3 Draw around the template on the reverse side of the fur. You need two pieces of fur for each ear. Place together with right sides facing and sew round, leaving a gap.

4 Turn the ears right side out through the holes you left. Sew the fur ears on to the headband, making sure they are in the correct position.

Cat

Use the instructions given previously in this chapter to make a pair of black furry ears. Dress up in a black catsuit and you will be the most glamorous, sleek pussy cat in town.

YOU WILL NEED
make-up sponge
water-based face paints
medium make-up brush
fine make-up brush
thick make-up brush
blusher

medium make-up brush

fine make-up brush

thick make-up brush

make-up sponge

water-based face paints

1 Using a damp sponge, apply a white base over the whole face. Using a medium brush, paint a border of black spikes around the edge of the face. You might find it easier to paint the outline first and then fill it in.

2 Paint a black outline around the eyes as shown in the picture and paint over the eyebrows.

3 Making sure the model's eyes are closed, fill in the eyelids and inside the black outline with a bright shade. This is a very delicate part of the face, so take care, and do not apply make-up too close to the eyelashes. Paint above the eyes.

4 Using a fine brush, paint a heart shape on the tip of the nose and a thin line joining the nose to the chin, avoiding the mouth.

5 Paint the lips a bright shade and then paint black whisker spots under the nose.

6 Using a thick brush, dust each cheek with blusher.

Animal Collar

This elegant and stylish collar will make any cat or dog look a million dollars.

YOU WILL NEED
tape measure
black velvet ribbon
scissors
silver fabric or cardboard
fabric glue
sequins
sewing needle and thread
press studs (snap fasteners)
 or a hook and eye fastener

scissors

ribbon

sequins

fabric glue

tape measure

press studs

1 Ask an adult or a friend to help measure your neck with a tape measure so that you know how long you need the ribbon to be, and cut it to this length. For the decoration, cut out six dots from silver fabric or cardboard.

2 Glue the spots on to the ribbon at equal distances from each other, making sure there is enough room between each one for a sequin. Leave them to dry.

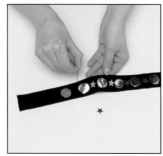

3 Sew on a sequin in between each silver spot.

4 Fold the ends of the ribbon over and secure them down with a dab of glue. Sew on the fasteners with a needle and thread and the collar is ready to wear.

Animal Accessories

These fun adornments will add the finishing touch to your cat or dog outfit.

YOU WILL NEED
templates for dog bone badge
  and fish pendant
cardboard
scissors
white glue
bowl
water
newspaper
paints
paintbrush
brooch pins
foil
hole puncher
ribbon

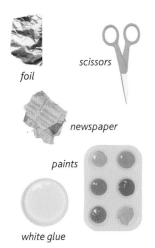

foil

scissors

newspaper

paints

white glue

1 Using the template for the dog bone badge, cut out a bone shape from a piece of cardboard. Cover with layers of pâpier-maché as described in the introduction.

2 To give the badge a more three-dimensional appearance, roll up balls of newspaper and stick them on to the bone. Cover them with strips of newspaper for a smooth finish. Leave the bone to dry.

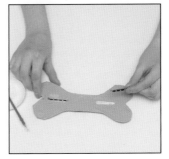

3 Paint the bone a bright shade and, when the paint has dried, add large dots in a contrasting shade. Leave to dry.

4 Using white glue, stick two brooch pins on to the back of the badge. Leave the glue to harden before trying on the badge or the brooch pins will come away.

5 Make the fish pendant in the same way except, instead of painting it, cover the fish and the fin in foil. You will need a hole puncher to make the hole for the ribbon.

Tiger

For a complete look, dress up in an outfit made from fake tiger fur and use the instructions at the beginning of this chapter to make a pair of matching furry ears.

YOU WILL NEED
make-up sponge
water-based face paints
medium make-up brush
fine make-up brush

medium make-up brush

fine make-up brush

make-up sponge

water-based face paints

1 Using a damp sponge, apply the base tone over the face.

2 Rinse the sponge, then stipple a darker shade of paint around the edge of the face, as shown in the picture above.

3 Sponge the chin and the area above the mouth white. Using a medium brush, paint the area around the eyes white as shown. You might find it easier to paint the outline first and then fill it in.

4 Using a medium brush, paint on the black markings around each eye, as shown, making sure each side is the same.

5 Using a fine brush, paint the tip of the nose black and paint a thin black line from the middle of the nose to the top lip. Paint the top lip black and extend the line at each corner of the mouth, stopping halfway down the chin.

6 For the rest of the markings, paint brushstrokes of paint across the face. To keep the design symmetrical, finish one side of the face first and then copy the design on to the other side.

Lion

The wilder your hair is the fiercer you will look. Try roaring and snarling in a mirror to see what different expressions you can make, but try not to frighten any of your friends or family. Complete the look by making a pair of ears as shown on page 19.

YOU WILL NEED
make-up sponge
water-based face paints
natural sea sponge
medium make-up brush
fine make-up brush or
   make-up pencil
lipstick brush
thick make-up brush

make-up sponge

*medium
make-up brush*

*water-based
face paints*

*fine make-
up brush*

*lipstick
brush*

*thick make-up
brush*

1 Using a damp sponge, apply the base tone over the face.

2 Using a natural sponge, dab a darker shade around the edge of the face as shown.

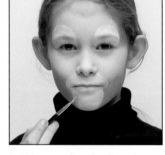

3 Using a medium brush, apply white make-up over each eyebrow to form an almost circular shape. Shade the area around the mouth and chin white.

4 Study the picture carefully so that you know where to paint the markings on the face. You might find it easier to outline some of them with a fine brush or make-up pencil first and then fill them in. Only paint the top lip at this stage.

5 Paint the bottom lip red.

6 Using a thick brush, dust the nose and middle of the forehead with a shade of brown. Use the template for the cat ears to make some lion ears to finish off your costume.

Spotted Dog

This funny dog's outfit is easy to make. Simply cut out circles of felt and stick them on to a pair of leggings and a T-shirt using fabric glue. Use the template and the instructions provided earlier to make a pair of spotted ears and a tail to match.

YOU WILL NEED
make-up sponge
water-based face paints
fine make-up brush
medium make-up brush

make-up sponge

water-based face paints

fine make-up brush

medium make-up brush

1 Using a damp sponge, apply a white base tone over the face. Gently sponge a slightly darker shade around the eyes.

2 Paint one eyebrow black and, using a fine make-up brush, paint a wiggly outline around the other eye to make a patch. Paint another patch outline on the side of the face. Paint the outline for a droopy tongue below the bottom lip.

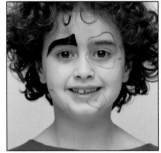

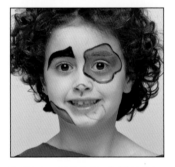

3 Using a medium brush fill in the patches grey and outline them in black. Draw the outline for the nose and a line joining the nose to the mouth.

4 Fill in the tongue red and outline in black. Paint a short black line along the middle. Fill in the tip of the nose pink and add a thick black line where the nose joins the mouth. Paint the middle of the top lip black. Paint black whisker spots under the nose.

28

Rabbit

This adorable little bunny is dressed all in white. As well as using the instructions provided earlier to make a pair of furry ears, you could also make a fluffy tail from cotton wool balls and stick it on to the T-shirt.

YOU WILL NEED
make-up sponge
water-based face paints
black make-up pencil
medium make-up brush
pink blusher (optional)
fine make-up brush

water-based face paints

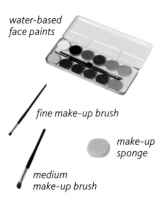

fine make-up brush

make-up sponge

medium make-up brush

1 Using a damp sponge, apply a white base tone over the face.

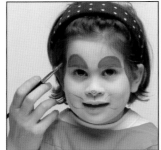

2 Using a black make-up pencil draw a heart on the tip of the nose, a circular outline above each eyebrow, a line joining the nose to the mouth and a circle on each cheek. Using a medium brush, fill in the marked area above the eyebrows grey.

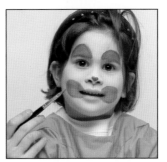

3 Paint the heart at the tip of the nose red and paint the cheeks pink with water-based face paints or pink blusher.

4 Using a fine brush, draw the outline of the teeth over the bottom lip. Fill them in with white make-up. Using a medium brush, paint the line joining the nose to the mouth black. Paint black whiskers above each eyebrow and on each cheek.

Bumble Bee

Buzz around in this striped outfit. Why not paint a pair of tights or leggings in the same style?

YOU WILL NEED
yellow T-shirt
newspaper
black fabric paint
paintbrush
paints
headband
paper baubles
scissors
milliner's wire
sewing needle and thread
black felt
fabric glue
black cardboard
pencil

FOR THE FACE
make-up sponge
water-based face paints
medium make-up brush

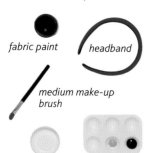

fabric paint　　*headband*

medium make-up brush

fabric glue　　*paints*

1 Place the T-shirt on a flat, wellcovered surface. Fill the T-shirt with flat pieces of newspaper. Paint black lines across the T-shirt and on the arms and leave the paint to dry. Turn the T-shirt over to the other side and continue painting the lines.

4 Fold a piece of black cardboard in half and draw the shape of a bee's wing, so that, when it is cut out and the paper is opened out, you will have two identical wings that are joined together. Carefully sew the wings along the fold on to the back of the T-shirt.

2 For the antennae, first paint the headband black and leave the paint to dry. Paint the paper baubles yellow and, when the paint has dried, paint a black line around each one.

3 Cut a length of wire, about 45cm/18in long. Bend the wire to fit the headband, making sure each piece of wire that will support the bauble is the same length. Sew the wire on to the headband and glue a strip of black felt over the wire for extra support. Carefully secure the baubles on to the ends of the wire.

5 For the face, use a damp sponge to apply a yellow base tone. Using a medium brush, paint a black line on the eyelids and under each eye. Paint a black spot on the tip of the nose.

Butterfly

When you wear this pretty outfit, gently move your arms to make the wings flap.

YOU WILL NEED

2.5m/2½yds milliner's wire
scissors
adhesive tape
netting in a pretty shade
sewing needle and embroidery
   thread (floss) in a bright shade
smaller pieces of netting in
   different shades
silver or gold elastic cord
headband
2 paper baubles
paints
paintbrush
white glue
glitter
felt
leotard and tights

white glue

headband

paper bauble

glitter

netting

1 Cut a piece of milliner's wire 2m/2yds long. Bend the ends together to make a circle. Secure the ends with a piece of tape. Pinch the two sides of the wire circle together and twist. The wire should now resemble a figure of eight.

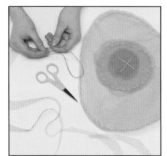

2 Place the wire frame between two pieces of netting and sew the frame on using embroidery thread. Trim away any excess net. Cut circles of netting in different shades and sew them on to each wing. Thread a loop of elastic cord on to the outside of each wing for the arms to slip through.

3 Paint the headband and each paper bauble a bright shade and leave them to dry thoroughly. Cut a short piece of wire and stick it into the bauble. This will make covering it in glitter much easier. Paint the bauble with a coat of glue and dip it into the glitter. Leave the glue to dry.

4 Cut a 45cm/18in length of wire for the antennae. Bend the wire to fit the headband, with each end of wire the same length at either side. Glue to the headband then glue on a piece of felt for support. Decorate the headband with glitter. Secure the baubles to the wire. Wear a leotard and pair of tights.

Mouse

Use the template and the instructions provided earlier to make a pair of furry mouse ears. Beware of cats and owls when you are wearing this costume as they like eating little mice!

YOU WILL NEED
make-up sponge
water-based face paints
black make-up pencil
medium make-up brush
thick make-up brush
pink blusher
fine make-up brush

water-based
face paints

make-up
sponge

fine make-up
brush

medium make-up
brush

thick make-up brush

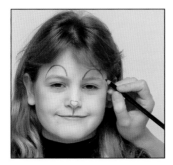

1 Using a damp sponge, apply a white base tone. With a black pencil, mark a pair of eyebrows above the model's own. Draw a heart on the tip of the nose, then a line joining the nose to the mouth.

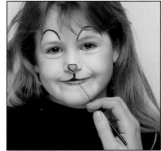

2 Using a medium brush, paint the area under the eyebrows and the eyes white. Paint the heart pink and the outlines of the eyebrows and the heart black. Paint a line that joins the nose to the mouth and continue on to the middle of the top lip, to form a triangle.

3 Using a thick brush, dust pink blusher on to each cheek.

4 Using a fine brush, paint the black outline of the teeth over the bottom lip. Fill in the teeth white. Paint on a few black whisker spots and whiskers.

33

Owl

In this design, large yellow owl eyes are painted on to your eyelids, so when your eyes are closed, it looks as though they are wide open.

YOU WILL NEED
thick make-up brush
water-based face paints
medium make-up brush
fine make-up brush
hair spray
hair clips

medium make-up brush

thick make-up brush

water-based face paints

1 Using a thick brush, paint a white area around each eye, leaving bare the area surrounding the eye.

2 Paint the rest of the face brown, except for the mouth, the upper lip and the tip of the nose.

3 Using a medium brush, apply red to the tip of the nose, the upper lip and the mouth.

4 Paint yellow on the eyelids and around the eye. Do not apply too close to the eyelashes. Using a fine brush, paint a black stripe across the top of each eyelid and a short stripe down the middle. Paint a black line around the red nose and mouth area and black streaks around the eye area.

5 Add feathery streaks around the eye area in yellow and white.

6 Brush the hair off the face into feathery tufts and secure it with hair spray and hair clips.

Monkey

For the complete monkey outfit make a pair of furry ears and wear brown clothes. You could even make a brown tail.

YOU WILL NEED
make-up sponge
water-based face paints
fine make-up brush
medium make-up brush

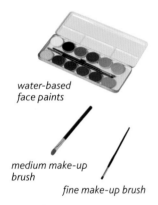

water-based face paints

medium make-up brush

fine make-up brush

make-up sponge

1 Using a damp sponge, apply a yellow base tone over the face.

2 Rinse the sponge, then dab a few darker shades around the edge of the face, blending them in with the base tone.

3 Paint the outline of the monkey's mouth using a fine brush. Use a medium brush to fill in the marked area with black.

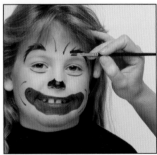

4 Paint the tip of the nose black and paint on a pair of eyebrows above the model's own. Using a fine brush, paint lines in between the eyebrows, under each eye and either of the mouth.

Panda

If you only have a few face paints, this is the perfect project for you. It is good for beginners as it is simple to do. Use the template and the instructions provided earlier to make a pair of furry ears to match.

YOU WILL NEED
black make-up pencil
make-up sponge
water-based face paints
medium make-up brush
fine make-up brush

*water-based
face paints*

*make-up
sponge*

*medium
make-up brush*

*fine make-up
brush*

1 Using a black make-up pencil, gently draw an outline around each eye as shown. Draw an outline across the tip of the nose.

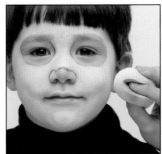

2 Using a damp sponge, apply a white base tone over the face, avoiding the areas you have just marked with the pencil.

3 Using a medium brush, paint the eyes and the tip of the nose black. Using a fine brush, paint a line joining the nose to the mouth and paint the lips. Paint small whisker spots either side of the mouth. Add black lines between the eyebrows.

Witch

This young witch looks like she's got a few tricks up her sleeve. She is wearing a cloak made from an old piece of fabric and long black nails.

YOU WILL NEED
tape measure
black fabric for hat
iron-on interfacing (optional)
pencil
scissors
sewing needle and thread
raffia or straw

FOR THE FACE
make-up sponge
water-based face paints
lipstick brush
fine make-up brush
thick make-up brush

black fabric

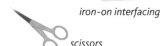

sewing thread

raffia

iron-on interfacing

scissors

1 For the hat, measure the width of your head so that you know how wide to make the rim. If the fabric needs to be stiffened, ask an adult to help iron a piece of interfacing on to the reverse side. Draw and cut out a triangle with a curved base. Ensure the rim measures the width of your head with a small allowance for sewing the fabric together.

2 With the right sides facing, fold the triangle in half to form a tall cone and sew along the side.

3 Make bundles of raffia or straw and tie a knot in the middle of each bundle. Sew each bundle around the rim of the hat leaving a gap at the front. The more bundles you sew on, the wilder the wig will be. Turn the hat the right way out.

4 For the face, use a damp sponge to dab the base tones over the whole face.

5 Using a lipstick brush, paint on wild black eyebrows. Paint a black line above the eyelashes. Paint a line of red under each eye and a black curve below it.

6 Add ageing lines with a fine brush (see instructions in the introduction). Build more tone on to the cheeks using a thick make-up brush. Paint the lips red, exaggerating the top lip.

Ghost

Spook your friends in this fabulous disguise. See how long it takes before they guess who you are.

YOU WILL NEED
old white sheet
scissors
sewing needle and thread
  or sewing machine
milliner's wire
black felt
fabric glue

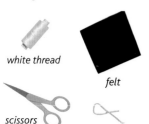

white thread

felt

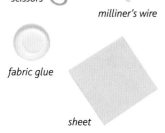

scissors

milliner's wire

fabric glue

sheet

1 Cut two pieces of sheet in the shape of a dome, making sure that the height of the dome is longer than you own height. Sew the two pieces together leaving an opening at the bottom. Sew another line of stitching parallel to the line you have sewn. This is to make a tube for the wire.

2 Thread the wire through the tube. Secure each end of the wire to the sheet with a few stitches.

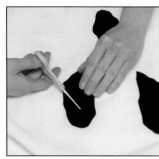

3 Cut out a mouth and pair of eyes from a piece of felt and glue them on to the sheet using fabric glue.

4 Cut small holes in the eyes and the mouth. Try the costume on and bend the wire to fit your body.

Egyptian Mummy

Make sure you wear a white T-shirt and a pair of white tights or leggings underneath the costume, just in case it starts to unravel!

YOU WILL NEED
old white sheet
scissors
sewing needle and thread
white T-shirt and leggings
   or tights

FOR THE FACE
make-up sponge
water-based face paints

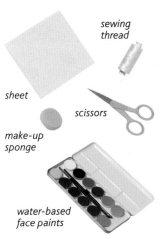

sewing thread

sheet

scissors

make-up sponge

water-based face paints

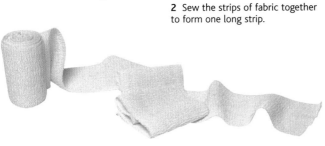

1 To make the costume, tear or cut strips of the sheet about 10cm/4in wide and as long as possible.

2 Sew the strips of fabric together to form one long strip.

3 For the face, use a damp sponge to apply a white base. Rinse the sponge, then dab light purple around the eye sockets. Wrap the fabric round the head first, leaving the face open. Wrap the fabric down the body.

4 When you get to the hands, go back up the arm, wrapping the fabric around. Do the same with the legs. When you have wrapped the whole body, sew the end of the strip to part of the costume.

Vampire

Dress all in black for this costume. Don't be surprised if you frighten your friends and family with your haunted face.

YOU WILL NEED
make-up sponge
water-based face paints
medium make-up brush
fine make-up brush
black make-up pencil (optional)
red make-up pencil
fake blood (optional)

water-based face paints

fake blood

fine make-up brush

medium make-up brush

1 Using a damp sponge, apply a base tone on the face. Rinse the sponge, then dab a slightly darker shade on the forehead, blending it with the base tone.

2 Using a medium brush, paint a black triangle in the middle of the forehead, one on either side of the face at the cheekbones and a small one at the bottom of the chin. You might find it easier to draw the outline for each shape first, to make sure they are symmetrical, and then fill them in.

3 Using a fine brush paint a pair of jagged eyebrows over the model's own. Again, you may find it easier to draw the outline first.

4 Paint the eyelids white and the area up to the eyebrows grey. Use the red make-up pencil to shade the area under the eyes.

5 Exaggerate the points on the top lip and fill in the lips black.

6 Paint the outline of long, pointed fangs under the bottom lip and fill them in with yellow. Dab fake blood or red make-up at the points of the fangs and at the corners of the eyes.

Martian

Try decorating an old pair of tights or leggings in a similar style to the T-shirt and give an old pair of shoes a 'space lift' with paint and glitter.

YOU WILL NEED
4 paper baubles
headband
paints
paintbrush
white glue
glitter
glitter glue
sequins
ribbon or elastic
T-shirt
felt in different shades
scissors
fabric glue
fabric paints

FOR THE FACE
make-up sponge
water-based face paints
stipple sponge
medium make-up brush
glitter gel
lipstick brush

make-up sponge

stipple sponge

medium make-up brush

lipstick brush

water-based face paints

1 To make the costume, paint the baubles and the headband and leave them to dry. Using contrasting shades, paint spots on the baubles.

2 Paint areas of the baubles with white glue and dip them into the glitter. Use glitter glue to make exciting shapes and patterns and glue on a few sequins. Try to create a different pattern on each bauble and try to make them look like little planets, if you like.

3 Glue three baubles on to the headband with white glue. For the necklace, glue the two ends of the ribbon or elastic into a small hole on the fourth bauble. Allow the glue to dry before trying on the accessories you have made.

4 To decorate the T-shirt, cut out two spiral shapes from felt and using fabric glue, stick them on to the T-shirt. Decorate the spirals with fabric paints and glitter glue.

5 For the face, use a damp sponge to apply the base tone. Using a stipple sponge, dab a slightly darker shade over the base tone to add some texture.

6 Using a medium brush, paint on a pair of wiggly eyebrows as shown. Using glitter gel in a contrasting shade, paint a spot on the tip of the nose.

7 Using a lipstick brush, paint a tiny mouth as shown, avoiding the corners of the mouth. Now put on your Martian T-shirt and baubles.

Frankenstein's Monster

Perfect your monster's walk when you wear this costume. This will really scare your friends.

YOU WILL NEED
make-up sponge
water-based face paints
thick make-up brush
medium make-up brush
fine make-up brush
black swimming hat

make-up sponge

water-based
face paints

fine
make-up
brush

medium
make-up
brush

thick
make-up
brush

1 Using a damp sponge, apply the base tone over the face. Rinse the sponge, then apply a darker shade, avoiding the mouth and the nose area. Finally, shade the cheekbones with a third shade.

2 Using a medium brush, paint the eyebrows black and darken the eyelids and the area under each eye.

3 Paint the lips black and, using a fine brush, paint fine black lines at either side of the mouth.

4 Using a fine brush, paint a black scar on the forehead and on the face. Put on the swimming hat, hiding your hair. Where the hat meets the forehead paint a jagged hair line.

Purple Monster

If you want to be a really gruesome monster, wear a set of rotten-looking plastic teeth. They can be bought from toy or joke stores.

YOU WILL NEED
make-up sponge
water-based face paints
fine make-up brush
medium make-up brush

water-based face paints

make-up sponge

fine make-up brush

medium make-up brush

1 Using a damp sponge, apply the base tone over the face. Dab a darker shade around the edge of the face and on the forehead, blending it with the base tone.

2 Using a fine brush, paint a pair of eyebrows slightly above the model's own. Paint the tip of the nose and paint on a droopy moustache just above the model's mouth. You might find it easier to sketch an outline for the shapes first and then fill them in.

3 Use a medium brush to paint on shapes. Start on one side of the face, then do the other side. This will ensure the design is symmetrical. Paint the lips the same shade.

4 Decorate the face with silver and purple spots and other details.

Skeleton

This is the perfect outfit for spooking your friends and family on Hallowe'en.

YOU WILL NEED
black leotard
white fabric paints
paintbrush
black leggings

FOR THE FACE
black make-up pencil
water-based face paints
medium make-up brush

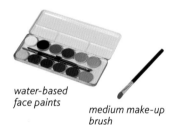

*water-based
face paints*

*medium make-up
brush*

paintbrush

fabric paint

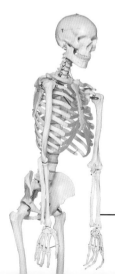

1 To make the costume, use fabric paints to draw on the outline of the skeleton's body, making sure the leotard is lying flat.

2 Paint the outline of the skeleton's legs on the front of the leggings.

3 Fill in the outlined areas with white on both the leotard and the leggings.

4 Using a black make-up pencil, draw a circular outline around each eye, a small triangle above each nostril, and a large mouth shape around the model's own mouth. Draw an outline around the edge of the face.

5 Using a medium brush, paint the face white, avoiding the shapes you have just drawn in pencil.

6 Paint the eyes, the triangles above the nostrils and the sides of the face black. Paint a thick black outline around the mouth and fill the mouth area in white. Divide the mouth into a set of ghostly teeth with black lines.

Zombie

You could dress in black to make this creepy character look even more scary.

YOU WILL NEED
make-up sponge
water-based face paints
thick make-up brush
medium make-up brush
fine make-up brush
fake blood (optional)

 make-up sponge

water-based face paints

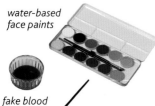

fake blood

fine make-up brush

thick make-up brush

medium make-up brush

1 Using a damp sponge, apply the base tone over the face, avoiding the area surrounding the eye. Use a thick brush to dust a darker shade on the forehead, around each eye and around the mouth, to create a bruised effect.

2 Using a medium brush, fill in the area surrounding the eye with a darker shade, then paint dark lines under the eyes and on the eyebrows.

3 Paint the lips a light shade and use a fine brush to paint on dark lines, so the lips look cracked. Using fake blood or red make-up, paint the corners so they seem to be bleeding.

4 Use a fine brush to paint the scar on the forehead.

Gremlin

This mischievous creature is all dressed in green.
Cover a green T-shirt with a piece of fur and wear
a pair of green tights.

YOU WILL NEED
tape measure
headband
fake fur
scissors
sewing needle and thread
fabric glue
felt
template for ears
pencil

FOR THE FACE
water-based face paints
medium make-up brush

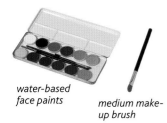

water-based face paints

medium make-up brush

1 Measure the length of the headband and cut the fake fur to fit. Sew the fur on to the headband, then sew or glue a strip of felt to the inside.

2 Using the template, draw and cut out two pieces of fur for each ear. With right sides facing, sew the two ear pieces together. Turn right side out and stitch on to the headband.

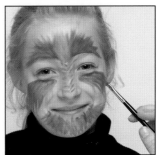

3 For the face, apply green areas with feathery brush strokes.

4 Paint a brown spot at the end of the nose and paint the lips the same shade, enlarging the top lip so that it meets the tip of the nose.

Dinosaur

*Dress up as a prehistoric monster with this
spiky camouflaged outfit.*

YOU WILL NEED
green fabric or felt
scissors
green polo neck or T-shirt
fabric glue
sewing needle and thread
fire-resistant wadding (batting)
headband
green paint
paintbrush
white glue

FOR THE FACE
make-up sponge
water-based face paints
stipple sponge
medium make-up brush

headband

sewing thread

fabric glue

fabric

wadding

scissors

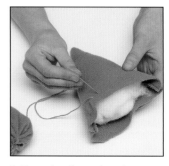

1 To make the costume, cut out lots of triangles, more or less the same size, from a piece of old green fabric or felt. You could use different types of green fabric if you don't have enough of one kind.

2 Starting at the bottom of the shirt, glue on the fabric spikes so that they overlap each other. Leave a circle in the middle of the shirt empty.

3 For each spike on the spine, you will need to cut out two triangles. Sew the two triangles together with right sides facing. Turn the triangles right side out and fill with wadding to make a spike shape. Sew a running stitch around the bottom edge of the spike and pull gently. This will draw up the threads and close the spike. Tie a knot.

4 Paint the headband green and leave it to dry. Cut a strip of green fabric about 10cm/4in wide and however long you wish it to be. Using glue, secure the strip on to the inside of the headband and leave to dry.

5 Sew the spikes on to the strip of fabric attached to the headband.

6 For the face, use a damp sponge to apply the base tone over the face. Using a stipple sponge, dab a darker shade over the base tone.

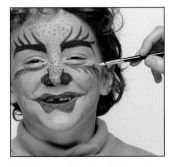

7 Using a medium brush, decorate the face. Paint on wild eyebrows, exaggerated nostrils, spots, big lips and markings under each eye.

Clown

Bounce around in this jolly outfit and entertain your friends and family. Decorate a hat and an old pair of shoes to match the bright costume.

YOU WILL NEED

6 self-cover buttons
scraps of fabric
template for clown button
pencil
felt in several shades
scissors
sewing needle and thread
old shirt
old pair of trousers (pants)
fabric glue
milliner's wire
broad ribbon
fabric for the bow tie
narrow ribbon

FOR THE FACE

make-up sponge
water-based face paints
black make-up pencil
medium make-up brush
fine make-up brush
thick make-up brush

fabric

sewing thread

buttons

scissors

milliner's wire

1 Cover each button in a different scrap of fabric. Using the template, draw and cut out a flower shape from a piece of felt and snip a hole in the middle of it. Fix the flower on to the back of the button and secure on the back. Sew the buttons on to the shirt and trousers.

2 Cut out large dots of felt and stick them on to the trousers with fabric glue. Thread a piece of milliner's wire through the waistband. Twist the two ends of the wire together to secure them.

3 Sew two separate lengths of ribbon on to the waist of the trousers to make a pair of braces (suspenders) Sew a covered button on to each brace.

4 To make the bow tie, sew two rectangular pieces of fabric together with the right sides facing, leaving a gap. Turn right side out and stitch the gap. Tie a piece of ribbon in a knot around the middle.

5 Tie the bow tie around the clown's neck under the shirt collar. For the face, use a damp sponge to apply a smooth white base tone.

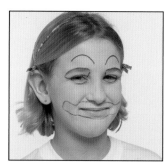

6 Using a black make-up pencil, draw the outline of a clown's mouth. Draw a pair of eyebrows above the model's own and gently mark an area around each eye, as shown.

7 Using a medium brush, paint the area around each eye with lots of shading and paint over the drawn eyebrows with a thick black line.

8 Using a fine brush, paint the mouth red, and outline the shape of the mouth In black. Using a thick brush, paint the cheeks a rosy red.

Ballerina

Show off your ballet steps in this pretty tutu. Make it the same shade as your ballet leotard.

YOU WILL NEED
2m/2yds netting in
   one shade
sewing needle, thread and
   dressmaker's pins
tape measure
wide ribbon for the waistband
narrow ribbon for the bows
scissors
matching leotard and tights

narrow ribbon

sewing thread

netting

scissors   wide ribbon

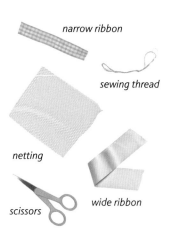

1 Fold the netting over lengthwise and sew a line of running stitch along the folded edge. Measure your waist. For a short tutu, fold over again, and secure with running stitches. Pull the thread to gather the netting to fit the waist and tie a knot or sew a few stitches to secure the gathers.

2 Pin the wide ribbon on to the gathered netting and then sew it on.

3 Using the narrower ribbon, tie about six small bows. Sew five bows on to the waistband.

4 To finish the costume, sew the last bow on to the leotard.

Fairy

Dress up in this sparkling outfit and make a special wish. For a magical effect, wear a white leotard and pin some tinsel in your hair.

YOU WILL NEED

2m/2yds netting
sewing needle and thread
scissors
tinsel
1.5m/1½yds white fabric
milliner's wire
silver elastic cord
garden cane
silver paint
paintbrush
silver paper or cardboard
adhesive tape
fabric glue
white leotard and tights

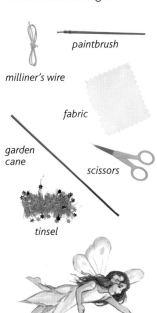

paintbrush

milliner's wire

fabric

garden cane

scissors

tinsel

1 Make the tutu as for the ballerina tutu, folding the netting lengthwise once only for a longer skirt. Sew a piece of tinsel on to the waistband. Cut out two pieces of white fabric for the wings, in a figure of eight. On the wrong side of one of the pieces of fabric, sew a separate length of wire around each wing.

2 Place the other piece of fabric on top of the first making sure the wrong sides are facing. Sew around the edge to secure the two pieces of fabric together.

3 Sew a loop of elastic cord on to each wing, near the middle. These will slip over the arms to support the wings on the body.

4 To make the wand, paint a cane silver and leave it to dry. Cut out two silver stars and tape the cane on to the reverse side of one of the stars. Glue the stars together.

Scarecrow

If you don't have any suitable old clothes of your own, visit a second-hand clothes store or rummage through piles of clothes at a local flea market. The older the clothes are the better the costume will be.

YOU WILL NEED
raffia
old felt hat
scissors
plastic toy mouse
glue
sewing needle and thread
old clothes, such as a jacket
   and trousers (pants)
scraps of fabric
orange cardboard
orange paint
paintbrush
elastic cord

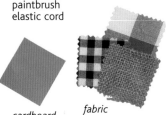

cardboard   fabric

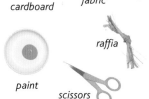

raffia

paint   scissors

1 Tie a few strands of raffia around the hat. Cut a fringe into the rim of the hat with a pair of scissors. Glue a plastic mouse on the top of the hat.

2 Tie bundles of raffia in a knot and sew the bundles around the inside rim of the hat, leaving a gap at the front.

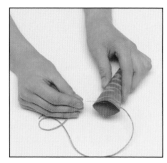

3 Cut ragged edges on the jacket and the trousers.

4 Cut scraps of fabric into squares and rectangles and sew them on to the jacket and the trousers.

5 To make the nose, cut a piece of orange cardboard into a cone shape. Roll the cardboard into a cone and glue it together.

6 Paint orange lines around the cone and leave them to dry. Make a small hole on either side of the cone and thread a piece of elastic cord through that will fit around your head. Tie a knot at each end of the elastic.

Angel

To make the tutu, follow the instructions for the ballerina, but sew a piece of tinsel on to the waistband instead of the ribbon. Make the wings the same way as for the fairy costume.

YOU WILL NEED
headband
2 paper baubles
silver paint
paintbrush
milliner's wire
tinsel
white glue
white leotard and tights

tinsel

headband

paper bauble

sewing thread

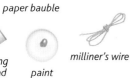
paint

milliner's wire

paintbrush

scissors

1 For the halo, paint the headband and the two paper baubles silver, then leave them to dry.

2 Bend a piece of milliner's wire in a circle and twist the ends together to secure them. Attach two separate lengths of wire about 7.5cm/3in long to the wire circle.

3 Wrap a piece of tinsel around the wire circle.

4 Glue the baubles to the headband and leave the glue to harden. Make a hole in each bauble and fix the ends of the wire into the holes with glue.

Devil

Make the devil a tail using an old red sock or one leg from a pair of tights. You could complete the costume with a trident and a set of false nails bought from a novelty store.

YOU WILL NEED
headband
tape measure
scissors
red felt
sewing needle and thread
template for devil horns
pencil
thick interfacing

FOR THE FACE
make-up sponge
water-based face paints
fine make-up brush
medium make-up brush
lipstick brush

headband

interfacing

sewing thread

scissors   felt

1 Make the ears as described in the animals chapter, covering the headband with red felt and using the template for the devil horns. Place the two pieces of felt together with right sides facing and sew round the edges, leaving a gap. Do the same to the other ear. Turn right sides out. Cut a piece of interfacing to fit inside each ear. Sew the ears on to the headband.

2 For the face, use a damp sponge to apply a smooth white base. Use a fine brush to paint a pair of eyebrows on top of the model's own.

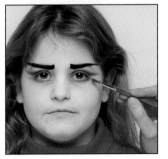

3 Using a medium brush, paint the eyelids a dark shade and paint the area under the eyes red. Using a lipstick brush, paint the lips red.

4 Paint a fiery flame on the model's chin and paint a similar design on the side of each cheek.

Robot

The fun part of this project is collecting all the bits and bobs to recycle. Ask your friends and family to help you collect interesting boxes, cartons and packages.

YOU WILL NEED

2 cardboard boxes
pencil
scissors
silver spray paint
cartons and containers made of
    cardboard and clear plastic
white glue
3 Christmas baubles
foil pie dishes
masking tape
a pair of old shoes
2 metal kitchen scourers
foil

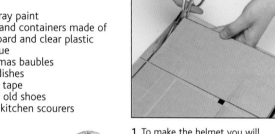

foil pie dish

metal kitchen scourer

Christmas bauble

white glue

egg carton

scissors

silver spray

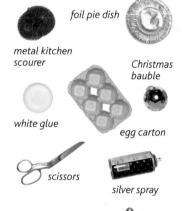

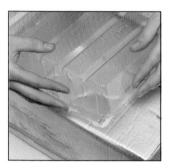

1 To make the helmet you will need a cardboard box that fits comfortably over your head. Draw a square on one side of the box and cut it out.

2 Ask an adult to help spray the box silver. You should do this outdoors or in a very airy room where the surfaces are well covered, to protect them. When the paint has dried, glue a clear plastic carton over the hole. Punch holes in the carton to let air through.

3 Decorate the box by gluing on some Christmas baubles and foil pie dishes.

4 For the body of the robot, you will need a large cardboard box. Draw and cut out a hole on the top of the box for your head and one on either side for your arms. Secure the edges of the holes with some masking tape.

5 Decorate the body of the robot by gluing on all the boxes and containers you have been collecting. When the glue has dried, spray the box silver, as in step 2. Leave the paint to dry completely before you try on the costume.

6 Spray a pair of old shoes silver and decorate them with a metal kitchen scourer or anything shiny. Finally, when you are dressed in your costume, ask a friend to wrap your arms and legs in foil to finish.

Astronaut

This space voyager looks all set for a journey to the stars and planets. Collect recycled containers to decorate the costume.

YOU WILL NEED
large balloon
white glue
bowl
water
newspaper
pencil
scissors
silver paint
paintbrush
foil pie dishes
foil
adhesive tape
piece of foam rubber
plain T-shirt
cardboard containers,
    such as fruit cartons
old pair of gloves (optional)

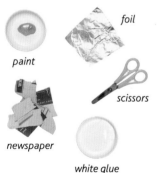

foil

paint

scissors

newspaper

white glue

1 To make the helmet, blow up a large balloon and cover it with about 10 layers of pâpier-maché as described in the introduction. Leave to dry.

2 When the pâpier-maché has dried, pop the balloon with a pin. Draw and cut out an opening for the face and remove the balloon.

3 Paint the helmet silver and then decorate with shapes cut from foil pie dishes.

4 Make a microphone from a piece of rolled foil and tape it securely to the inside of the helmet. To make the helmet more comfortable to wear, glue a piece of foam rubber to the inside at the front.

5 Decorate a plain T-shirt by gluing on containers and foil pie-dishes.

6 Make the arm and leg shields from cardboard containers. Fruit cartons have been used here. Paint the cartons silver and bend them to make a tube. Glue the edges together. If you have an old pair of gloves, paint them silver.

Sunflower

Dazzle your friends with this bright, cheerful headdress. Wear yellow and green clothes to complete the costume.

YOU WILL NEED
pair of compasses
cardboard
scissors
ribbon
adhesive tape
pencil
yellow paper
white glue
black paint
paintbrush

FOR THE FACE
make-up sponge
water-based face paints
medium make-up brush

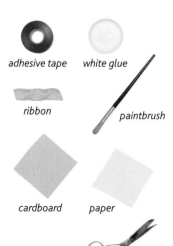

adhesive tape   *white glue*

ribbon   *paintbrush*

cardboard   *paper*

scissors

1 To make the costume, use a pair of compasses to draw and cut out a circle from a piece of cardboard. Draw and cut out a circle in the middle big enough for your face to show through.

2 Make a slit either side of the circle and thread a piece of ribbon through. Secure the ribbon down with a knot and a piece of adhesive tape.

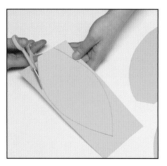

3 Draw a petal shape on to yellow paper, and use it as a template for the others. You will need about 42 petals for a full sunflower. Cut out the petals.

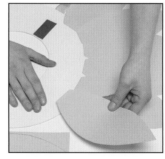

4 Starting at the edge of the cardboard circle, glue on the petals so that they overlap each other. When you have covered the outer edge start on the second row and finish off in the middle of the circle.

5 Paint black marks around the middle of the sunflower and leave the paint to dry. When you are ready to wear the flower, tie the ribbon around your head in a bow.

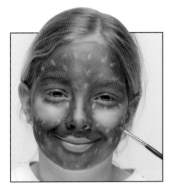

6 For the face, use a damp sponge to apply a brown base tone. Use a medium brush to paint yellow spots on the base tone. Paint the lips the same shade.

7 Paint yellow highlights under each eye and on the nose.

Pumpkin

You will certainly win the biggest pumpkin competition if you wear this outfit.

YOU WILL NEED
headband
green paint
paintbrush
scissors
green fabric
sewing needle and thread
  or sewing machine
stuffing (batting)
3m/3yds orange fabric
fabric tape
milliner's wire
safety pin
elastic

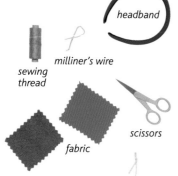

headband

sewing thread

milliner's wire

fabric

scissors

elastic

1 To make the pumpkin stalk, paint the headband green and leave it to dry. Cut out two pieces of fabric for the stalk and sew them together with the right sides facing. Leave a gap and turn right sides out. Fill the stalk with stuffing and sew up the end. Sew on to the headband.

2 To make the pumpkin body, first fold over the two long sides of the orange fabric and sew a line of stitches on each long side to make a 1.5cm/½in tube for the elastic.

3 Sew lengths of fabric tape widthwise on the reverse side of the fabric. You will need to sew on about five lengths of tape, positioned equal distances apart.

4 Thread a length of milliner's wire through each fabric tape tube. Bend the ends over and sew them on to the tape.

5 With the right sides facing fold the fabric in half widthwise, and turn so that the tubes for the elastic are at the top and bottom. Sew the shorter sides together.

6 Attach a safety pin to the elastic and thread through the top and bottom tubes. Pull the end of the elastic to gather the fabric and tie a double knot. Before you try on the costume, bend the wires so that they are curved, to make a full, round shape.

Carrot

For the complete outfit, dress up in an orange T-shirt and leggings and, if you have an old pair of shoes, paint them orange.

YOU WILL NEED
pencil
green cardboard
scissors
glue

FOR THE FACE
make-up sponge
water-based face paints

green cardboard

white glue

scissors

1 Draw lots of differently shaped leaves on green cardboard and cut them out.

2 Cut two strips of green cardboard 5cm/2in wide and long enough to fit around your head. Glue the leaves along one of the strips.

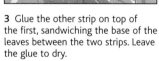

3 Glue the other strip on top of the first, sandwiching the base of the leaves between the two strips. Leave the glue to dry.

4 Curve the cardboard to fit around your head and glue the two ends of the strip together. Leave the glue to dry before trying the headdress on.

5 For the face, use a make-up sponge to apply an orange base tone all over.

Genie

You can make your own baggy pantaloons by following the instructions provided in the introduction.

YOU WILL NEED
a pair of shoes
glitter paint
paintbrush
glue
glittery braid
scraps of fabric
baggy trousers (pants)
    or pantaloons
scissors
fabric glue
fabric for the cummerbund
tape measure
sewing needle and thread
    or sewing machine
fabric for the turban
feathers

FOR THE FACE
make-up sponge
water-based face paints
medium make-up brush

feather

sewing thread

fabric

fabric glue

paintbrush

glittery braid

scissors

1 To make the costume, paint a pair of shoes a sparkling shade and leave to dry. Stick a piece of glittery braid around the side of each shoe.

2 Making use of scraps of fabric, cut out lots of stars and glue them on to a pair of baggy trousers or pantaloons using fabric glue.

3 Measure your waist for the cummerbund, allowing an extra 25cm/10in so that you can tie the fabric at the back. Sew two pieces of fabric together to the required length with the right sides facing, leaving an opening at one end, and turn it right side out. Sew up the end.

4 Cut out some more stars from scraps of fabric and glue them on to the cummerbund with fabric glue.

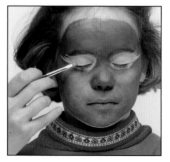

5 For the face, use a damp sponge to apply the base tone, avoiding the area around the eyes. Paint the area around the eyes a bright shade.

6 Tie the turban around the head, tying a neat knot on the top of the head. Tuck the loose fabric underneath the turban. Place a few bright feathers on the top of the turban to decorate.

Dragon

To make a pair of ears follow the instructions provided for the devil horns.

YOU WILL NEED
red fabric
scissors
sewing needle and thread
pair of children's red tights
newspaper or wadding (batting)
elastic

FOR THE FACE
make-up sponge
water-based face paints
stipple sponge
medium make-up brush

newspaper

sewing
thread

tights

elastic

wadding

scissors

1 To make the tail, cut two triangles of fabric for each spike. Sew them together, leaving one side open. Fill each spike with crumpled-up newspaper or wadding. Sew a running stitch around the opening and pull the threads to gather up the end. Tie a knot to secure.

2 Cut one leg off the tights and fill it with crumpled-up newspaper. Sew up the end and pull the thread tight.

3 Sew a loop of elastic to the end of the tail, long enough to fit comfortably around your waist.

4 Sew the spikes on to the tail.

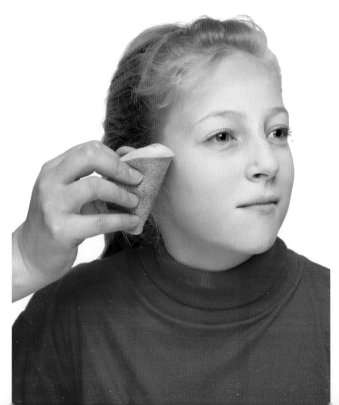

5 For the face, use a damp make-up sponge to apply a base tone.

6 Using a stipple sponge, stipple a dark shade on the base, avoiding the area around the eyes and the mouth.

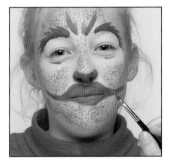

7 Using a medium brush, paint a large mouth, eyebrows, the tip of the nose and marks on the forehead.

Gypsy

Wear your brightest clothes to go with the accessories and make up your own gypsy dance.

YOU WILL NEED
cardboard
scissors
newspaper
white glue
bowl
water
paints
paintbrush
glitter
sequins
fabric for the head scarf
   and shawl
sewing needle and thread
   or sewing machine
braid
pom-poms

paintbrush

paints

braid

glitter

newspaper

sewing
thread

white glue

sequins

scissors

cardboard

1 Cut a strip of cardboard to fit comfortably around your wrist and about 5cm/2in wide. Bend the cardboard to make a bracelet and glue it in place.

2 Scrunch up small balls of newspaper and glue them on to the bracelet. Cover the bangle in three layers of pâpier-maché as described in the introduction, and leave it to dry thoroughly in a warm place.

3 Paint the bangle using lots of shades and leave the paint to dry.

4 Paint dabs of glue on the bangle and sprinkle on the glitter. Glue a few sequins on for extra sparkle and decoration. Leave the glue to dry before trying on the bracelet.

5 For the head scarf, sew two triangular pieces of fabric together with the right sides facing. Leave a gap and turn right side out. Sew up the gap.

6 Sew a strip of braid along the longest side of the scarf. Make a larger, but similar, scarf to go around your neck and sew pom-poms along the sides.

Cowboy

Find a hat and a toy gun to complete this costume.
Round up your friends and have fun.

YOU WILL NEED
tape measure
felt for the waistcoat
    (US vest)
scissors
sewing needle and thread or
    sewing machine
templates for pocket
pins
fabric glue
template for sheriff badge
pencil
cardboard
foil or silver paint
paintbrush
safety pin
strong adhesive tape

foil

felt

scissors

adhesive tape

safety pin

1 Measure from the nape of your neck to the length required, and cut two squares of felt to this size. Cut one in half lengthwise for the two front pieces. With the right sides facing, sew these to the back along the shoulders. Sew the sides together leaving gaps for the arms.

2 Turn the waistcoat right side out. Use the template to cut out two felt pockets. Pin them on the front. Use the template to cut out two contrasting pieces of fabric and glue them on the top of the pockets. Sew on to the waistcoat with bright thread.

3 Using a pair of scissors, snip along the bottom of the waistcoat to make a fringe.

4 To make the badge, use the template to draw around and cut out a piece of cardboard. Cover in foil or paint silver. Decorate with a silver '5', and silver spots on the tip of each point. Tape a safety pin on to the reverse.

Native American

You can buy the feathers for this costume from most good fabric stores. You can make the skirt from felt with an elastic waistband.

YOU WILL NEED
tape measure
wide ribbon
scissors
feathers
felt
fabric glue
sewing needle and
    embroidery threads (floss)
wool (yarn)
narrow ribbon

FOR THE FACE
water-based face paints
medium make-up brush

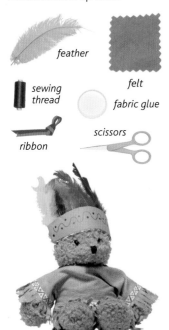

feather

felt

sewing
thread

fabric glue

ribbon

scissors

1 Measure around your head with a tape measure, allowing a 5cm/2in overlap and cut the wide ribbon to this length. Arrange the feathers in the middle of the ribbon on the reverse side. Cut a strip of felt the same width as the ribbon and glue it on to the feathers. This will help to secure them in place.

2 Sew a few lines of decorative stitching along the ribbon, using bright embroidery threads. With the right sides facing, sew the two ends of the ribbon together.

3 To make each braid, you will need about 45 equal strands of wool. Tie a piece of wool around one end of each bundle. Ask a friend to help you with the braiding by holding one end of the bundle tight while you braid. Tie a piece of ribbon in a bow at the end of each braid.

4 Sew or glue the braids on to the inside of the headdress, so that they lie either side of your face. For the face, use bright shades to paint three zigzag lines on each cheek.

Pirate

This pirate is dressed for an exciting voyage across the ocean. Glue a skull and crossbones on to a plain T-shirt and tie a scarf around your neck to complete the costume.

YOU WILL NEED
black felt
scissors
template for skull and crossbones
pencil
white felt
fabric glue
sewing needle and thread
elastic
dressmaker's pins

FOR THE FACE
fine make-up brush
water-based face paints

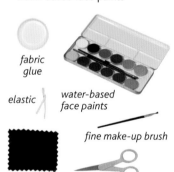

fabric glue

water-based face paints

elastic

fine make-up brush

felt

scissors

1 For the hat, cut two equal pieces of fabric, following the shape in the photograph. Using the template for the skull and crossbones draw around and cut out the shapes from white felt. Glue them on to the front of the hat with fabric glue.

2 Sew the two pieces of fabric together around the edge.

3 To make the eye patch, cut out two pieces of black felt the same size. Cut a piece of elastic long enough to go around your head. Trap the elastic in between the two patches and pin in place with a dressmaker's pin.

4 Sew around the edge of the patch to secure the elastic.

5 For the face, use a fine make-up brush to paint on a moustache.

6 Use your fingertips to rub on red and purple to make a bruised scar.

7 Paint a line down the middle of the scar with a fine brush.

Prince

To make a sword, follow the instructions given for the knight's costume. The cloak was made from a piece of fabric found at a flea market and was decorated with a piece of tinsel to match the crown.

YOU WILL NEED
tape measure
pencil
scissors
cardboard
silver paint
paintbrush
bright foil paper
glue
glitter
tinsel
fabric for cloak
safety pins

bright foil paper

scissors   *white glue*

glitter   *tinsel*

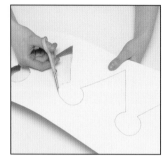

1 Measure around your head with a tape measure so that you know how big to make the crown. Draw and cut out the crown from a piece of cardboard.

2 Paint the cardboard silver and leave the paint to dry thoroughly. Cut shapes out of bright foil paper and glue them on to the crown. Paint dots of glue on to the shapes and sprinkle on some glitter.

3 Glue a piece of tinsel around the rim of the crown and leave the glue to dry.

4 Glue the ends to fit on your head and leave the glue to dry. Pin the fabric to your shoulders as a cloak.

Princess

If you have always dreamed of being a beautiful young princess, and imagined living in a castle, dress up in this costume and maybe your dream will come true.

YOU WILL NEED
tape measure
fabric for hat
fabric interfacing (optional)
pencil
scissors
sewing needle and thread
chiffon fabric
wool (yarn)
narrow ribbon
braid

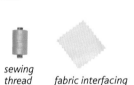
sewing thread

fabric interfacing

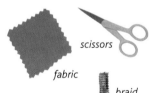
fabric

scissors

braid

1 Measure the width of your head, so you know how wide to make the hat's rim. If the fabric needs to be stiffened, iron a piece of interfacing on to the reverse side. Draw and cut out a triangle with a curved base that matches the width of your head, with an allowance for sewing together. Sew a hem around the rim and, with the right sides facing, fold the triangle in half, trapping a piece of chiffon fabric at the point of the cone.

2 Sew the cone together. Turn right side out.

3 Following the instructions for the Native American, make a pair of braids and tie a piece of ribbon in a bow around the end of each one. Sew the braids on to the inside of the hat, so they lie either side of the face.

4 Sew a piece of braid around the rim of the hat, and arrange the chiffon fabric so that it trails down the side like a veil.

Hippy

Be loving and laid-back in this bright flower-power costume. Search flea markets and second-hand stores for vibrant clothes to wear with the accessories. Go completely wild and paint a flower on your cheek.

YOU WILL NEED
template for flower pendant
pencil
scissors
cardboard
newspaper
white glue
bowl
water
paints
paintbrush
hole puncher
ribbon
fabric or old scarf
scraps of felt in various shades
sewing needle and thread
buttons
tissue and crêpe paper sheets
garden canes

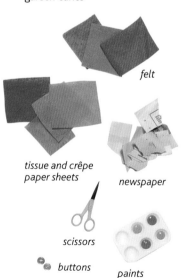

felt

*tissue and crêpe
paper sheets*

newspaper

scissors

buttons

paints

1 Use the template to draw around and cut a piece of cardboard in the shape of a flower. Scrunch up small balls of newspaper and glue them in the middle of the flower.

2 Cover the flower in three layers of pâpier-maché as described in the introduction and leave to dry thoroughly in a warm place for several hours or overnight.

3 Paint the flower in lots of bright shades and leave to dry. Using a hole puncher, punch a hole in one of the petals, then thread a piece of ribbon through the hole.

4 For the headband you will need a band of bright fabric or an old scarf. Cut out different shaped flowers from bright felt. Sew the flowers on to the headband and sew a button on to the middle of each flower.

5 To make a vibrant bouquet of flowers, first cut out lots of shapes in tissue and crêpe paper sheets. Starting with the largest petal at the bottom, layer the petals on top of each other, piercing a hole through them with the garden cane.

6 Roll a piece of tissue paper with glue and place it in the middle of the flower on the stick. Fan out the petals to finish off.

Knight

Have a pretend battle with your friends in this shiny suit of armour.

YOU WILL NEED
cardboard
scissors
foil
black felt
glue
foil paper in several shades
template for helmet
pencil
silver paint
paintbrush
template for body shield
hole puncher
ribbon

paint   *white glue*

scissors

foil paper in several shades

foil

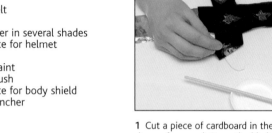

1 Cut a piece of cardboard in the shape of a sword. Cover the blade in silver foil. Cut two pieces of felt to fit the handle of the sword and glue them on. Decorate the handle with diamond shapes cut out of foil paper.

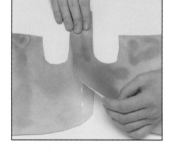

2 To make the helmet, use the template to draw and cut two equal pieces of cardboard. Paint these silver and leave to dry. Glue the two pieces together as shown in the picture.

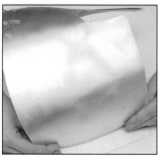

3 When the glue has dried, fold the helmet so that it curves. Glue the sides together. Hold the helmet together while the glue dries. To make the body shield draw round the shape, then flip it to complete the other half. Do this for the front and back pieces and cut them out.

4 Paint the two pieces silver. When the paint has dried, glue the two pieces together at the shoulder seam. Cut a foil paper cross and glue it on to the front of the shield. Punch a hole on either side of the body shield and thread a piece of ribbon through. Tie a knot to secure.

Wizard

Wave the magic wand and conjure up some secret spells.
Look in flea markets for a piece of fabric to make the cape.

YOU WILL NEED
tape measure
fabric for hat
fabric interfacing (optional)
scissors
sewing needle and thread
silver fabric
fabric glue
templates for wizard's pendant
pencil
cardboard
foil
silver ribbon
double-sided adhesive tape
garden cane
paint
paintbrush
tinsel

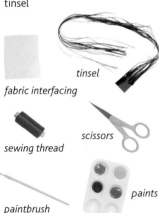

fabric interfacing

tinsel

sewing thread

scissors

paintbrush

paints

1 Measure the width of your head with a tape measure so that you know how wide to make the rim of the hat. You may need to ask a friend to help. If the fabric needs to be stiffened, iron a piece of inter-facing on to the reverse side. Ask an adult to help you. Draw and cut out a triangle with a curved base, making sure the rim measures the width of your head with an allowance for sewing together. Hem the bottom and, with right sides facing, fold the triangle in half to make a cone. Sew along the side. Turn the right side out and stick on silver fabric stars with fabric glue.

2 To make the pendant, use the template to cut out a cardboard star. Cut two circles of cardboard of the same size to make the backing. Cover both circles and the star with foil. Attach the ribbon to the back of the circles with a piece of adhesive tape.

3 Roll up strips of foil and place them on the reverse of one of the foil circles. Glue the other circle on top to trap the foil strips and secure them in place.

4 To make the wand, first paint a garden cane and leave it to dry. Stick a piece of shiny tinsel around one end of the stick with adhesive tape.

Super Hero

Be a hero for a day and make your very own costume.

YOU WILL NEED
cardboard
scissors
foil
foil paper in various shades
glue
silver cardboard
ribbon
adhesive tape
leotard or catsuit
2m/2yds fabric
sewing needle and thread

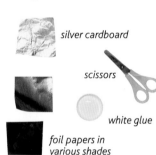

silver cardboard

scissors

white glue

foil papers in
various shades

1 To make a wristband, cut out a cardboard triangle and cover it in foil. Cut a smaller triangle in foil paper and glue it on to the triangle. Cut out the letter 'S' in silver cardboard and glue on to the triangle. Cut a strip of silver cardboard 5cm/2in wide and long enough to fit around your wrist. Glue to make a band and glue on the triangle. Make another the same way.

2 To make the waistband, cut a piece of cardboard to fit around your waist. Cut a cardboard circle and cover it in foil. Cut a star from foil paper. Glue it on to the circle. Cut out the letter 'S' in cardboard and glue it on to the star. Glue the circle on to the waistband.

3 At each end of the waistband, attach a piece of ribbon with adhesive tape. To make the headband, cut a strip of silver cardboard that is long enough to fit around your head when the ends are joined.

4 Cut a circle in foil paper. Cut a smaller circle in a different shade. Glue it to the middle of the larger circle. Cut out a silver letter 'S' and glue it on the circles. Cut a smaller 'S' in foil paper and glue it on to the silver 'S'. Make a cape as opposite.

Super Heroine

Impress your friends and family with your heroic powers and dress up in this futuristic costume.

YOU WILL NEED
cardboard
scissors
foil
foil paper in various shades
white glue
silver cardboard
ribbon
adhesive tape
bright cardboard (optional)
leotard or catsuit
2m/2yds fabric
sewing needle and thread

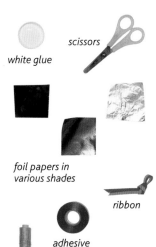

white glue

scissors

foil papers in various shades

ribbon

adhesive tape

sewing thread

silver cardboard

red fabric

1 Make the wristband, waistband and headband as for the Super Hero's outfit.

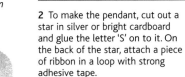

2 To make the pendant, cut out a star in silver or bright cardboard and glue the letter 'S' on to it. On the back of the star, attach a piece of ribbon in a loop with strong adhesive tape.

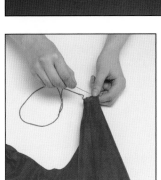

3 To make the cloak you will need a leotard or catsuit. Sew one end of the fabric on to the leotard shoulder straps.

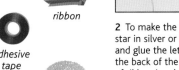

4 Where the fabric joins the straps, glue on silver cardboard triangles.

TEMPLATES

Some of the projects in this book need templates. You can either trace them directly from the book, or enlarge them to the size required. After all, not all kids are the same size! To double the size of a template, make a grid twice as large as the one below. For instance, if one square equals 2.5cm/1in, then draw a grid with 5cm/2in squares. Then copy the diagram square by square. If you wish to make the template larger still, enlarge the grid accordingly. Alternatively, simply enlarge using a photocopier.

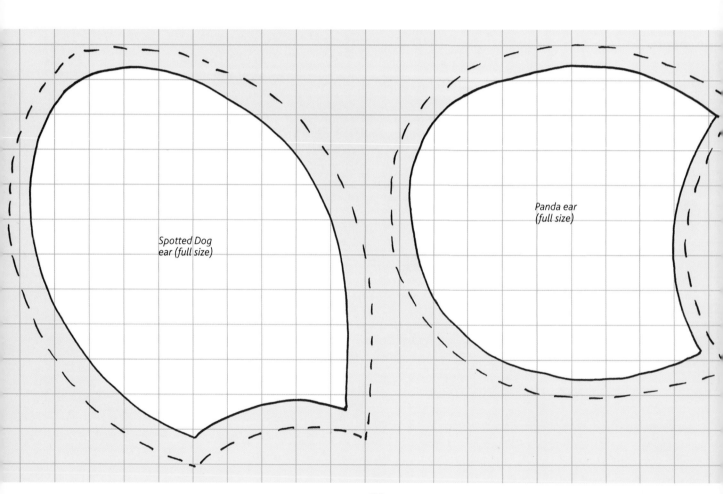

Spotted Dog ear (full size)

Panda ear (full size)

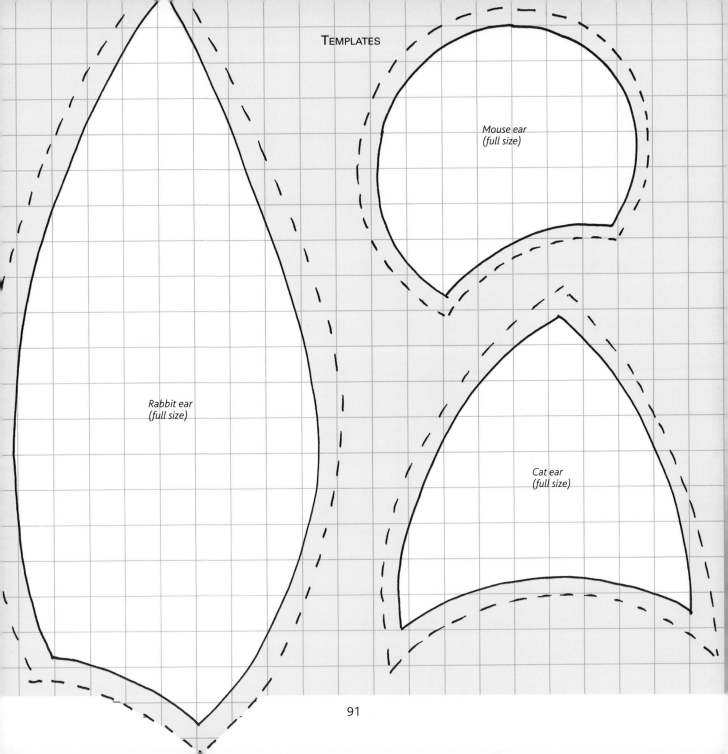

Mouse ear
(full size)

Rabbit ear
(full size)

Cat ear
(full size)

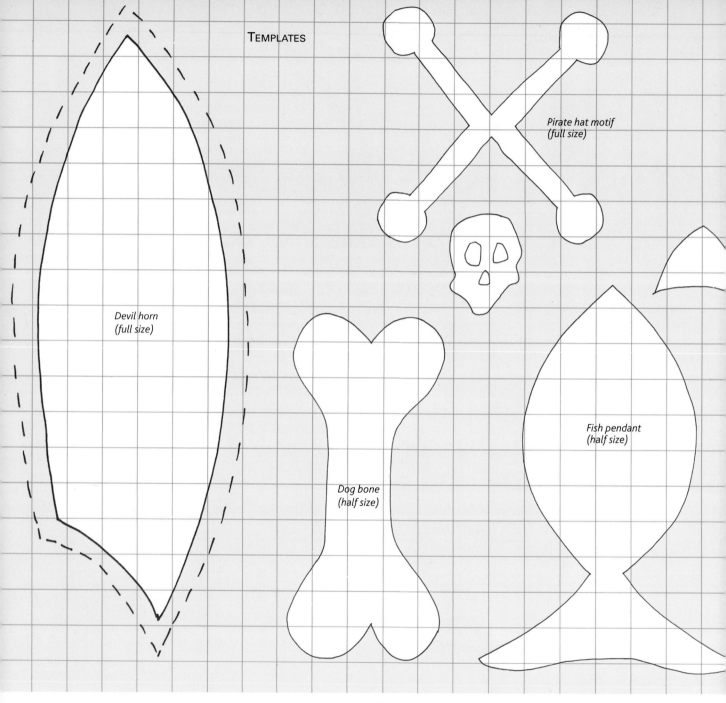

TEMPLATES

Pirate hat motif
(full size)

Devil horn
(full size)

Dog bone
(half size)

Fish pendant
(half size)

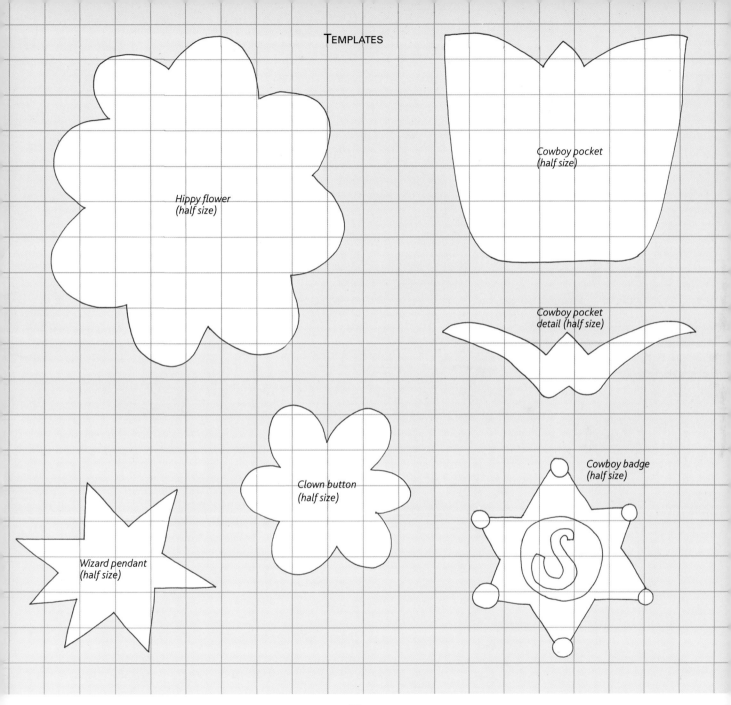

Hippy flower
(half size)

Cowboy pocket
(half size)

Cowboy pocket
detail (half size)

Clown button
(half size)

Cowboy badge
(half size)

Wizard pendant
(half size)

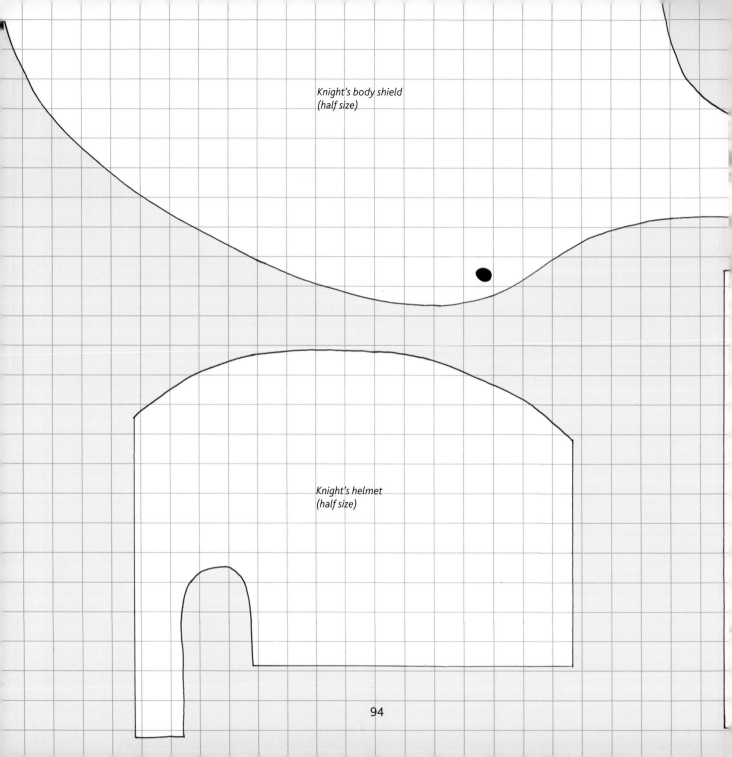

Knight's body shield
(half size)

Knight's helmet
(half size)

94

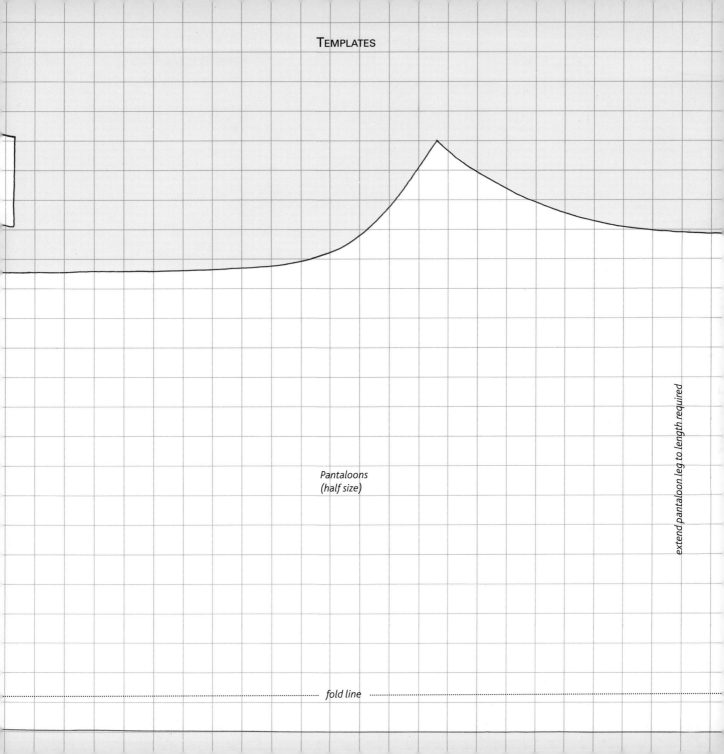

Pantaloons
(half size)

extend pantaloon leg to length required

········· *fold line* ·········

INDEX

A
Adhesive tape, 8
Ageing face, 17
American, native, 79
Angel, 60
Animals: bumble bee, 30
butterfly, 32
cat, 20
collar, 22
ears, making, 19
lion, 26
monkey, 36
mouse, 33
owl, 34
panda, 37
rabbit, 29
spotted dog, 28
tail, making, 18
tiger, 24
Armour, 86
Astronaut 64

B
Ballerina, 56
Base, applying, 16
Baubles, 8
Blood, fake, 10
Braid, 8
Brushes: eyebrow, 10
make-up, 10, 15
paintbrushes, 8
Bumble bee, 30
Butterfly, 32
Buttons, 8
clown, template, 93
covering, 12

C
canes, garden, 8
Carrot, 70
Cat, 20
ear, template, 91
Child's make-up kit, 10
Cleanser, cold cream, 10
Cleansing towels, 10
Clown, 54
button template, 93
Cold cream cleanser, 10
Collar, animal, 22
Cotton swabs, 10
Covered elastic
cord, 8

Cowboy, 78
badge template, 93
pocket detail, 93
pocket template, 95
Crayons, make-up, 10
Crêpe paper sheets, 8
Cross stitch, 13

D
Decorative stitches, 13
Devil, 61
horn, template, 92
Dinosaur, 52
Dog bone: papier-mâché, 23
template, 92
Dog, spotted, 28
ear, template, 90
tail, 18
Dragon, 74

E
Ears: making, 19
templates, 90, 91
Egyptian mummy, 41
Elastic cord, covered, 8
Elasticated waistband, 12
Eye make-up,
applying, 15
Eyebrow brush, 10

F
Face painting materials, 10
Face, ageing, 17
Fairy, 57
Fake blood, 10
Feathers, 8
Felt, 8
Fish pendant
papier-mâché, 23
template, 92
Fixative, make-up, 10
Frankenstein's monster, 50

G
Garden canes, 8
Genie, 72
pantaloons, 13
Ghost, 40
Glitter, 8
Glitter gel, 10
Gremlin, 51
Gypsy, 76

H
Hair: temple white, 10
Headbands, 8
ears on, 19
Hessian, 8
Hippy, 84
flower template, 93

K
Knight, 86

L
Lion, 26
Lips, painting, 17

M
Make-up: ageing face, 17
base, 16
brushes, 10, 15
crayons, wax, 10
fixative, 10
handling brushes, 15
kit, child's, 10
lips, painting, 17
palette, 10
pencils, 10
pots, 10
removing, 17
shading, 16
Martian, 44
Materials and equipment, 8
Milliner's wire, 8
Monkey, 36
Monsters: Frankenstein's, 50
purple, 47
Mouse, 33
ear, template, 91
Mummy, Egyptian, 41

N
Native American, 79
Netting, 8
Newspaper, 8

O
Owl, 34

P
Paintbrushes, 8
Paints, 8
Palette: make-up, 10
plastic, 10

Panda, 37
ear, template, 90
Pantaloons, making, 13
Paper, various shades of, 8
Papier-mâché, 14
pendant and badge,
23, 94
Pencils, make-up, 10
Pirate, 80
hat motif template, 92
pantaloons, 13
Plastic palette, 10
Plastic teeth, rotten, 47
Pots, make-up, 10
Press studs
(snap fasteners), 8
Prince, 82
Princess, 83
Pumpkin, 68
Purple monster, 47

R
Rabbit, 29
ear, template, 91
Ribbons, 8
Robot, 62
Running stitch, 13

S
Safety pins, 8
Scarecrow, 58
Sewing thread, 8
Shading, 16
Skeleton, 48
Soft tissue, 10
Sponges, 10
Spotted dog, 28
ear, template, 90
tail, 18
Stitches, decorative, 13
String, 8

Sunflower, 66
Super hero, 88
Super heroine, 89
Sword, 82, 86

T
Tail, making, 18
Templates
cat ear, 91
clown button, 93
cowboy badge, 93
cowboy pocket, 93
devil horn, 92
dog bone, 92
fish pendant, 92
hippy flower, 93
mouse ear, 91
panda ear, 90
pirate hat motif, 92
rabbit ear, 91
spotted dog ear, 90
tracing, 14
wizard pendant, 93
Temple white, 10
Tiger, 24
Tracing template, 14
Tutus, 56, 60

V
Vampire, 42

W
Waistband, making, 12
Wax make-up crayons, 10
Wire, milliner's, 8
Witch, 38
Wizard, 87
pendant template, 93

Z
Zombie, 46

ACKNOWLEDGEMENTS
The author and publishers would like to thank the following
models and their parents for their contribution:
Alex, Alice, Anthony, Clare, Faye, Helen, Jade, Jessica, Joe,
Joshua, Kelly, Kirsty, Lucy, Otis, Patrick, Rosie, Sophy, Tanya,
Timothy, Zoe and Zosia. Special thanks to Screenface, 24
Powis Terrace, London W 11 1JH for providing the pots of
make-up in the Fardel range on page 11.
The author and publishers would also like to thank Caroline
Thompson for her help in the studio.